Table of Contents

About ERC 860

To keep the tracking of the clients, ERC 860 gets used with allowing the custodian smart contracts with creating chains. The interface remains standard with having the hierarchy of level two construction. The management of asset remains with the coupons which get provided over the tickets during the digital monitoring in high value. The exchange value can be up to grading certificates of diamonds.

The recognition of ERC860 has been popular with the cryptocurrencies and the blockchain community. The implementation of the program keeps the clients work with the purpose on board with the architectural and hierarchical manner. The demand of clients work with their methods and how well they are able to accommodate with the framework which gets developed through the ERC860. The contracts of custodians are held by the creator and then functions get established through the help of smart contracts and the clients which are associated with smart contracts.

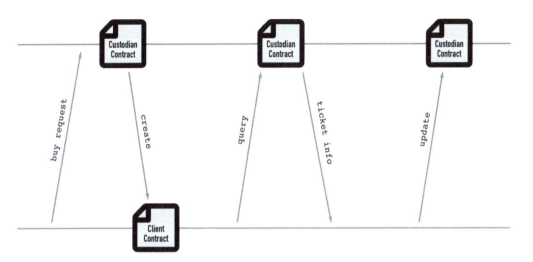

Coding for ERC 860

```
function transfer(address _to, uint256 _amount) returns (bool
success);

function transferFrom(address _from, address _to, uint256 _amount)
returns (bool success);

function balanceOf(address _owner) constant returns (uint256
balance);

function approve(address _spender, uint256 _amount) returns (bool
success);

function allowance(address _owner, address _spender) constant
returns (uint256 remaining);

function totalSupply() constant returns (uint);
```

The functions which are mentioned in the coding can be read by the experts who deal with blockchain and the ethereum. These allow the user to operate over the ethereum easily and they can work with it smoothly through following the commands on the image above.

Finding the Good in ERC860

With ERC860 there are certain things which you are able to get which cannot be found in other nodes of blockchain. You are able to get the independence which is flexible to handle. The contracts over the clients help in getting associations directly through the states which get shared and held over the contracts. The attacks may face over the loss which can be independent than other variable which is held over the cryptocurrencies. The single contract keeps track with the interface of attack and manages it well so that it does not spread over the system.

The upstream control is near to zero with the smart contracts and there will be no knowledge shared with the custodians or the clients. The addresses over the contract are able to keep the records with having controls over it sufficiently. As having the new entity will provide you benefits, there will be flexibility over the cause of getting the input of new smart contract. The compatibility with ERC20 will be easier through the new contract along with keeping some of the limitations under consideration.

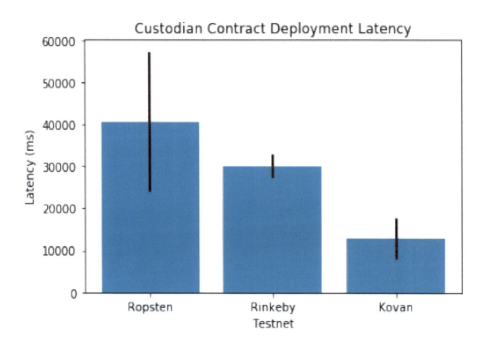

The extended form of ERC721 can be known as ERC860 with having multiple other implementations which can have their own specialty. The tokens get used for the purpose of independence with having resistance to fraud. The compatibility with keeping the flexibility under control is one of the biggest advantage which comes through when one is dealing with the token ERC860 rather than all the other standardized tokens.

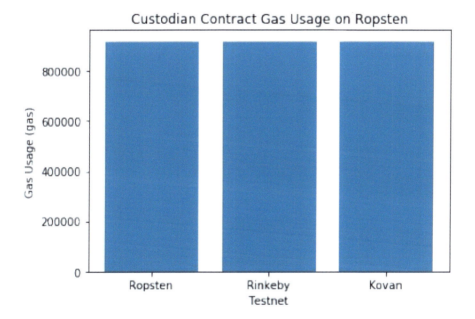

Custodian Contract Gas Usage on Ropsten

Helpful Ledgers over Blockchain

The right source of using ERC 860 is through the ledgers which are available over the blockchain platform for everyone to view. The only thing which is in the matter that it cannot be changed as the changes get saved in the server. No one is able to access the server which is why the cryptocurrencies are considered as one of the most centralized rules of the interactions. There are stores which keep in the establishments which are under the trusts and the parties are able to recognize it well too.

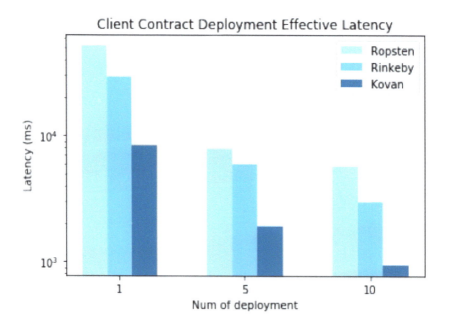

The right source of capabilities which are there for the in cognition will be held over the functions which get performed with the help of centralized system. The smart contracts play a huge rule in the ethereum as they are the under the decentralized rules of blockchain process. Having the right establishment of trust will be there for the functions keeping the sophistication. With keeping in mind that the demand will be there to have the data accessed, you have to make sure that the storage remains with keeping the demand high and you will be able to rule within the timely manner.

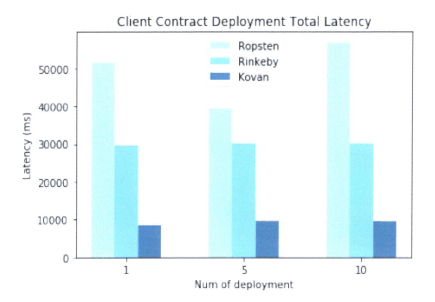

Keeping in the related interactions within the time and you have to get through the architecture, make sure that you keep the smart contracts aligned. With knowing over the functions, you have to keep the demand over execution. The parties are able to comprehend within the manner of time that blockchain will be responsible for all the information keeping in the considerations.

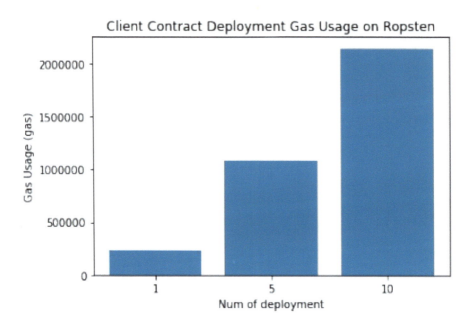

Client Contract Deployment Gas Usage on Ropsten

You have to keep the parties aligned with having the right interactions and keeping the rules under the lines as well. The proposing action of the time will be there for the types of manner which will be over the contracts.

You have to make sure that the clients are able to get over the custodians so that they keep the storage within the right data access as well. The exchange of the policies will be there to keep the storage over the smart contracts which can keep the access of the data hard for anyone to keep the demand.

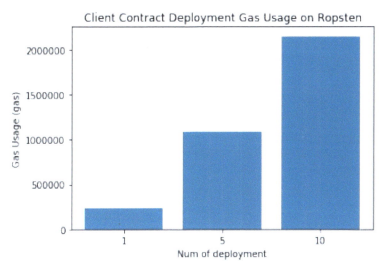

The interaction within the time over the messages will be there for you to keep the composition of two times with keeping the centralization on the exchange time. You will have to keep the demand under the line to know that the custodians are able to play their role well throughout the system in making sure that things are on the right track.

Understanding of ERC 860 Through Blockchain

Getting the blockchain access was not easy at first when it emerged in 2008. With the new technologies on the parts, there are some of the cryptocurrencies which are over the ledger to store new transactions. The transactions which can be incurred by the new ethereum or the employed decentralized systems.

There are some of the storage which is there for the actions over the storage of transactions and people are in doubt because of that because they are not able to find the relevant information for it. The usual content which seems to have the pointers will be back on the storage with keeping the transactions over the right side of it.

Once the process becomes easier, the contracts tend to shrink and find up the building of the capabilities. There are some of the users which are above all the blockchain and they are having the splendid attacks over the platforms. To guarantee that, the malware actions or the malicious activities on the account are all management by the security of SSL by the platform.

The scripts are saved over the server which no one is able to change except for a few people who have the admin control. The system works completely on the demand of the clients as there is no upper or lower management which is dealing with it.

Whereas, as it is made, there are some of the restrictions which you may face while you are trying to go against the system. It will not allow to you do the transaction which has not been activate or is unusual for the system to manage.

Therefore, having the benefit of bitcoin will keep the cryptocurrency of the blockchain which will be centralized over the transactions. With knowing the right sense of cryptocurrencies, there are some of the users which are able to store the track of all the occurring transactions.

The developed capabilities of the bitcoin can keep the limitations over the scripting and there will be programs which can be held as there are trees and the pointers which you can manage easily over the bitcoin. As usual as it sounds, the spending over the bitcoin can be larger and there are some of the users which will be able to keep the cryptocurrency on the usual experience with the help of new cryptocurrencies.

The content cannot be explained with the help of actions but the implementation will matter as the fact that you have to deal with certain limitations when you are dealing with all the accounts information.

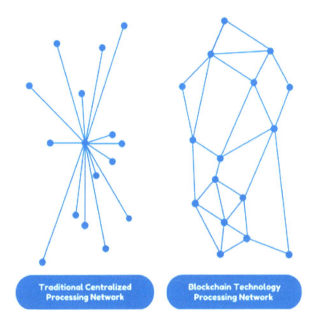

Traditional Centralized Processing Network

Blockchain Technology Processing Network

All the additional information should be provided on the end by knowing the designs and the credits which are under the roll for the management. The program and its development works with the script which you will have to deal with when you are playing around the ERC 860. There are some of the topics which keep the upper level under the state that you have to be variable about the level which is not serving as the rules around it.

You need to keep the management over the surface with knowing that the coupons will be there for the tracing actions and commodities which will be available on the right hand coupons above it. There can be set of examples which you will be able to find and get the right access for it among keeping the certifications which are not on the roll.

Blockchain Tokens

BlockchainHub

Currency Aspect

Cryptocurrencies are fungible stores of value that can be transferred P2P without a bank or any other middle man.

Fuel of the Network

A Token is needed to pay for usage of the network:

- **Bitcoin** (transactions)
- **Ether** (computing power)
- **Sia** (file storage)

Tokens are fuel of network used to reward stakeholders for network services and make network attack resistant.

Economic Rulesets

Network Economics

Stakeholders of the network (Miners, devs, exchanges, token holders, etc.) are incentivized to contribute to the network by being rewarded with a stake in the network (the token). The theory: better individual work -> better the overall performance of network -> more attention -> price of the token will rise. This dynamic might also lead to temporary overvaluation of token price.

Creating the Tokens through Blockchain

When you have the variables which are concrete and having the solutions for the ruling refined ideas then the contracts work through the system to gain the insights. The manageable actions have to be recorded by the transactions so that the variables are stable and it is able to find the level certified actions for it.

The smart contracts which are there for the level shown on the ticket are able to judge about the seller which is there for the ownership of the client and user relationship. When the smart contracts get exchanged, the contracts are able to keep the tickets under considerations so that they are able to deal with the way of ticketing and assigns the right regulations for it.

How to create a blockchain transaction

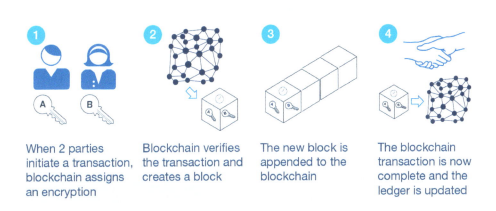

When 2 parties initiate a transaction, blockchain assigns an encryption	Blockchain verifies the transaction and creates a block	The new block is appended to the blockchain	The blockchain transaction is now complete and the ledger is updated

The assets are able to keep the coupons on the right track knowing that the supervision is there, you will be finding the ownership on the right custodian ways of passing onwards with the help of clients which can be transferred on the right track. You can also share the information on the basis of the distribution so that you do not have to wait for the creation of the ticketing over the management system.

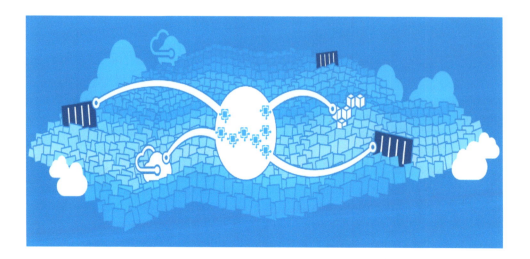

When you have the customers in line, you will be able to find relevant information about the ideas which work for you and the alignment of the tickets. Keeping the right management of tickets will help you keep the experimentation of the ideas which will surely increase the security of the chances and have the transaction security on the way for you.

The right source of information which you have to realize is to keep the contracts over the board knowing the usage of the discussion. The proposition of the architecture will be there for you to have the update over it and surprisingly you will be able to define the right process for it. Keeping the network over the language and you will be finding the explored side of it with the smart contracts. The knowledge can be gained as the random process is dealt with all the information and you will be finding the right source of information along the way.

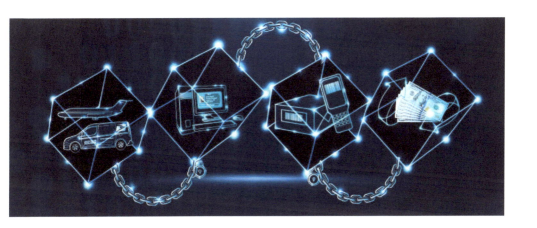

The fashion in which you will be dealing with is the right form of language you have to pursue. There is the side of knowledge which will be provided on the basis of the language will perform as the time is shared among all. The smart contract is based over the purchase of the tickets updated over the retrieval of the programs which you tend to participate.

About ERC 875

The rise of ERC 875 has been on peak since a while. In the world of cryptocurrency, the blockchain got its immutably strong chain which is over the ERC 875. The main breed for the ethereum is through the popularity which it gained in some time. The network has been pushed with the limits to get the high fees in return.

There are some of the blockchain which are not in the limit yet has their downsides which can be streamlined as well. The downside does not work over the limits with having fees which are above the networks and pushed over the while.

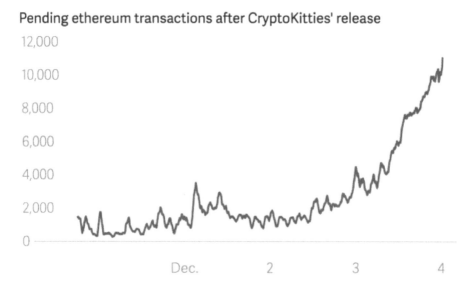

Pending ethereum transactions after CryptoKitties' release

The release of ERC 875 has been over the tokens which can be taken for the standardized procedures. There has been the implementation over the tokens which can be taken over the ethereum and with that, the rise has been tremendous since a while. The crypto kitty works with the non-fungible tokens which can be unique and able to remove the tokens without any limits. The effective results have to be shown with the help of ERC 875 and there are some of the drawbacks which they have to face as the time passes down.

The strains which can occur over the network can be only way that you have to exchange the token by turns. You cannot simply exchange them all of a sudden and in the bulk. There has to be the raise of the kitty over the time and should be able to produce more links to it over the networking issue. Similarly, there are some of the offers which you have to intake with the help of smart contracts through this ethereum. The change has to be settled with the help of keeping the details in manner so that the place for the market can be taken into consideration. The decentralized system works with having the kittens which are there for the official usage only. There are some of the transfers which you can intake for the massive trading and help in keeping the usage aligned. The main standards which has been used over the centralized system can be as the counter receives them with the passage of time. There can be some of the methods which you can use and keep the tokens under the line of fungible items. You can address some of the main features under ERC 875.

Coding ERC 875

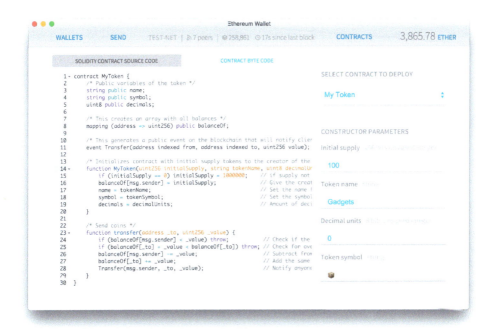

Here is the list of some of the main features which might seem to be exciting for you when you start using the ethereum 875.

A lot of Transfer

Keeping in mind that this ethereum requires your attention and have the tokens which can get transferred in a while. There are savings which can be brought to the index and have meaning of bringing in the budget. The tokens which can be used over the network are aligned with the transactions which need to be there for the specifications. The massive use of this ethereum keeps the work aligned having the index in place as well.

Safe Trading with Being Inexpensive

Beside all the trading which goes along with it, there are some of the decentralized parts of the system which can be under the construction. The involvement requires the transactions to be there for the bid who is going to make them and someone would be waiting out there to get the transaction done. It gets attached automatically with the receiver and then there is less time for the wait. If the transactions get sold individually then there are chances that you will be paying for the orders within the line. You have to keep in mind that the orders are there but the changing situations will be kept under the line. With the transactions and orders which are there for the support, you have to manage the system within the settings. The system works inexpensively for the ones who are regular over the blockchain platform.

The main source of cryptocurrency can be served as the major problem which needs to be addressed over the period of time. There are some of the updates which can be made with the interest and have the right meaning to it. You have to make sure that the transactions are aligned with the help of the appropriate receiving at the end. There are some of the payers which can get the alignment over the board and you have to get the order aligned. The buyers are able to get the process done within few time and have to manage the system with order.

About ERC 1155

The concept of blockchain came over the internet few years back and gained popularity all over the world in just some time. The first ethereum was brought about three years ago with having the complete tuning over the developers for the machines. The major portion of it consists with the smart contracts which are there in the form of token ethereum. Basically smart contracts have the abstract name of tokens instead which gets used on the blockchain platform. It is similar to owning anything valuable over the internet or digitally to have complete control of it.

The fungible tokens which are known under the ERC 20 tend to play the role of single types for the blockchain. The property which can be in the form of commodity or good have the units which get measured along the interchange. We can take the example such as finding the equivalent of gold in one kilogram with pure gold or in the form of ingots or coins. Gold does count under the fungible items with having majority of the part through cryptocurrencies.

The games on blockchain have some of the new tokens which include the token of ERC 1155 along the way with having the non-fungible tokens used. The unique unit works as the number which needs to be under the items which are collectibles. Having the blockchain success as the kitties will also incur with the games over blockchain where it has majority of clients engaged in this process every day.

Need of Token 1155

Having the start of the year, the tokens which were working over the standards tend to give the access to the games which were only mainstream. The items would not work with all the games and the users would find it hard to gain the compatibility. The token which was created about a year ago and took the inspiration from ERC 721 was the ERC 1155.

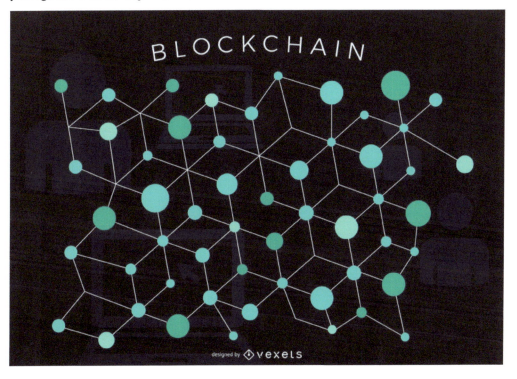

The design of token 721 was followed over ERC 1155 to create it and make it user friendly for the clients. There are more than 30,000 items within the Runescape game and above 90,000 items in the World of Warcraft game. They keep on switching with having the items under the skins of thousand users which are easy to locate. The problem which may exist with the tokens is through the design meant to keep over the separation.

Why ERC 1155 Created?

There are blockchain which carried away the items and having the contracts which work separately. The deployment with the tokens is one of the main things which bothered the contracts separately while they are on blockchain platform. So basically it will be similar being on a new software or computer every time you have to switch between the games. Any applications which you want to use will have to get the access through the new computer. It can be quite a hassle process due to which the convenience of ERC 1155 has been created.

So the token which gets made over the blockchain has to keep the existence in place with having developers to deploy the entire smart contracts. The complete deployment of smart contract is necessary with making the code which contains the information about contracts overall. The users have to work with the tokens having different numbers and places which are over the decimals. It can be different every time so the same code can be used multiple times as well.

The relation with blockchain is simply direct when it is about ERC 1155. The nodes which are distributed among the codes of tokens have the life of eternity. The alive surface makes the wastage of data with analyzing over the size which is of the state itself. There are more than 70,000 tokens which get explored through the blockchain over EnjinX. The transfers are done through the logs with having deployment of many ethereum at one time since the year of 2015.

A single hit over the game of blockchain has more than 90,000 items in it. So you can imagine that how much deployment gets done when there are tokens which serves as the contracts and have to work with it when it is not compatible. It would be hard to manage it on the practical side when the studio game does not respond. With having the new token with the contract along single one, the tokens will be easily distinguished within the states. The configurations have been taken over the data which will be there for the collection purposes. There are governing tokens which are possible for the minimization along with keeping ERC 1155 for the users and for the game lovers.

The process of getting something or having steps along with it are known to be atomic swap. These are the tokens which get exchange for the intermediary reasons and have the right existing designs which can be taken along the swapping reasons for the games. Getting along with the process requires steps which you have to clear in order have the right process of swapping between the tokens which are relevant and helpful.

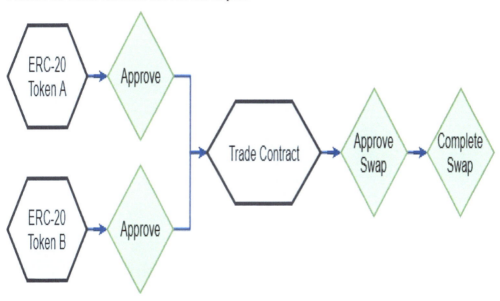

Life of Tokens

The tokens which come along have to be added over the type of trade which can be used as a step further for the contracts. There are smart contracts which are needed in order to show the steps which require certain types of approval for the ERC 1155 to appear on blockchain so that you are able to play the games certainly in a smooth way.

Keeping in mind that the trading does not coordinate and have to be among the separate tokens which can be related to the ERC 721 as the design has been similar for both of them somewhat. The swapping of the tokens is there for the crypto design which can be taken along the superiority and having a chance to keep the ERC 1155 along the way with a clear indication that it will allow the amounts whether there are any swapping program occurring or not.

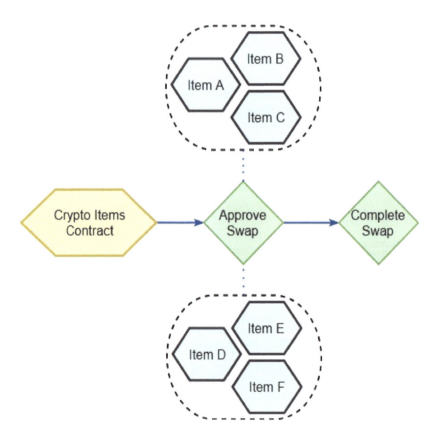

Coding ERC 1155

```
vim ExampleToken.sol

pragma solidity ^0.4.4;
import "./StandardToken.sol";

contract ExampleToken is StandardToken {
 string public name = "ExampleToken";
 string public symbol = "EGT";
 uint public decimals = 18;
 uint public INITIAL_SUPPLY = 10000;

 function ExampleToken() {
  totalSupply = INITIAL_SUPPLY;
  balances[msg.sender] = INITIAL_SUPPLY;
 }
}
```

Multi Steps Transfers

Keeping in mind that when you are out for the grocery and have the separate cart for it, there are some of the things which you have to certainly keep in mind. With keeping the items along the way and having the groceries on the way, you will be able to keep the right check over it with knowing how to deal with it within the right time.

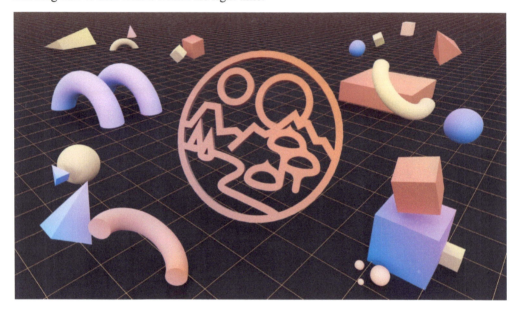

If you are purchasing a certain grocery, it is obvious that you will have to swipe the card for the payment, the receipt which you will get as the payment proof will help you in future if there are any troubles with the account and it can continue like that. The process of the receipts is never going to end because it provides the security to the store owner and the user to have the proof of buying something from a certain place.

Keeping in mind that when you always shop, even if you have the amount in the form of cash, it does not deficit you with the manner of having the continuation with it. So make sure that you get the right receipt and the single begging offer will be there for you to continue with the right manner of shopping either online or if you are at the brick store.

This is the reason how you can relate for the ERC 1155 to be working on your end that you have the proof of all the purchases for your own security. If there is a single recipient, that can be send to the single transactions which will have the items reduced over the time. Having the price fall, there is going to be a great amount of time which will be having the items on the preferred system.

The items keep on moving up till the recipients which will be there to have the reduction over the congestion and the ethereum gas when it is available for the users to pool in. When you have the time to get the savings out of it, it will be there for your help to get rid of any problem which will be existing in the time for you to keep the options for security open for yourself.

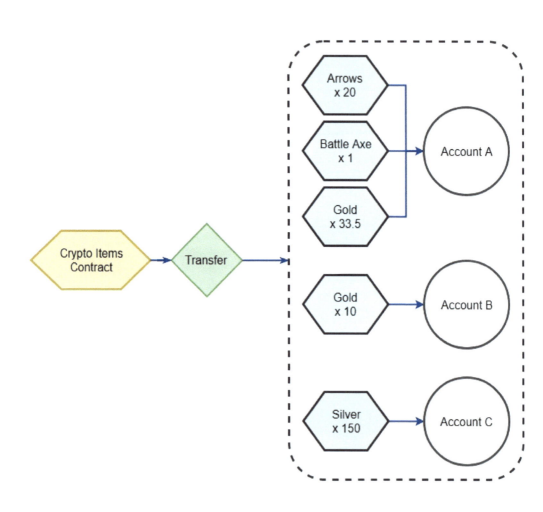

Having the right form of process really helps with the ERC 1155 so that you are able to perform all the functions in the right manner. The right following of the parameters and keeping the approval system on the trade will be helpful for you. So keep in mind that when you are dealing with such ethereum, there is a process of approval, trade and the melt which will be there for you to keep the transactions simple and approving for you. The right parameters will be there keeping the approval between the time of 100-200 meters which are operational within the smooth operations.

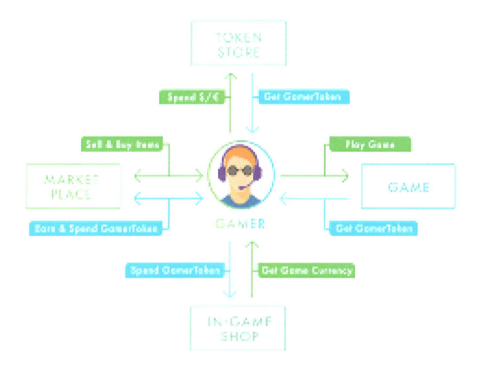

So have the items ready and when you have two of the main things which are there for you to keep in manner, you can have the operations running at that time. There are some functions which will be available and have the right meaning to the source of action. So make sure that the single element which is there for you will be there for the supply and you will be able to reduce each of the actions which will be having the performance on the right form of items which are fungible or not.

Fungible Items

Within this ethereum, you do have to deal with the fungible items which are focused over the collectibles of games. There may be a time when you would require both on the end and have the games on the modern sides. You can easily access the modern games which are there for the items keeping in mind that these items will be secure to handle and you will be running the system smoothly.

The right blockchain and the item should be able to get the collectibles on the route so that you can play within the right items and have the kits along with it. There can be some of the games which need to be held as the inventory goes through and you will be able to manage it easily with keeping in mind that you have to work with the right ammunition so that you are over it easily. One of the most common things within the games over the blockchain pattern are known to be the fungible and non-fungible items which can be on the time across your own time.

The senses which are used over the manner with keeping quantities entitled are the necessary units which you can hold. The right of trading and the action are there for the units to be kept under consideration. The necessary items which are there for the items and the units increased will be there for the armor and you will have to work with the items which are there for the right users. The quantities can be large enough to have the right source and among all, there can be some of the history which is attached to it.

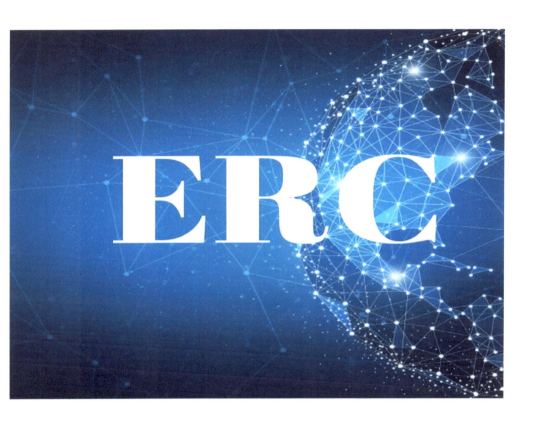

The dependence upon the right weapons will be there for the simple functions and you will have to deal with the independence which is there for the armors. You have to keep the designs within the history of unique independence knowing that these items will be there for the non-fungible items. The history of keeping the unique governing opens will be certainly there for you to have the copy of the issues which will not be over the right time.

Single Transactions

There are certain games which are designed over the time and you have to keep the attachment within the organization in the right manner. You need to work within the timely tokens so that all the advantage can be taken from these weapons along the time. You do not have to worry about the tokens necessarily but just the simple steps of counting it off would be a better option for you to deal with it.

There are some of the items which you will not like only because there will be dependence of too many games on one server. With having the single detachment, you will be able to find the source to it easily with understanding the mechanisms on the same side. Keeping the dependence over the time will be able to keep the use of it within large quantities and you will be finding it on the right way to keep it easily on the units which are there for you under the line.

With having the substantial ways, you will be likely to carry a lot of games which will be there over the simple item and the games will not be armored within the timely manner. The only design of the game will be there for the weapons which are used on the games which are played on the Warcraft or the warrior games.

To keep the right attachment with the games, you will be able to find the right source of it with the items which are there and not having the fungible times over the right weapons to deal with. You will be able to cope up with the limited times of the contracts which are there and having the single times will be keeping the copies which are there on the unique level of the information.

Without having the ERC 1155, you will not be able to keep the single contracts on the deal with keeping and having the items aligned. You will be able to keep the tokens with you along with having the types of compatibility which will be aligned over the mixable solutions for you to handle on the very end.

The right approval of the system will be there for the combination and you will be there for the index having others to keep the solutions for it. With creating a lot of information for the time, you will be able to reach the units under the measurement of having the dependency on each of the times which will be there for you.

The items which are based on the crypto will keeping the combinations of the survivals which will be there for you to keep the things aligned. The time of the tokens will be keeping under the solutions will be different types of solutions which can be handled. Keeping some of the compatibility will be there for the cases which are under the units of keeping index strong.

You will be able to find the relevant information which will be having thousands of information to keep the compatibility along the way to keep the case stronger. There will be times when you will find the cases on the unit separately but that will be useful for you since you will be dealing with each case on the separate ends.

With having the right amount of information for the machine gun and other unique social games, you will be able to find the tokens easily without any dealing and the information. The contracts are there for the information that you have to keep the transfers and there can be fungibles which are excitingly over the tokens and fungible items. There are trades and some of the mixtures which work through the items and tokens will be held as there are multiple solutions to it.

Having the right amount of tokens will be the powerful grid which you will be able to manage and compare over the right timings. You will be able to discuss some of the measures which will be there for you to handle it easily. Keeping the discussions with the right information will be there for tokens to keep the aligned under the manner that you will be able to deal with it in the efficient and wise manner.

The standards should be compared with the upgraded option which is there for the tokens and you will be finding immense amount of information which can be carried away easily with the mixture of tokens which are fungible and non-fungible.

By keeping some of the tokens under the line, there are smart contracts which play a huge role in it. The right timings and the behavior has to be there for the experience and efficient users to be opened. Keeping the storage of the items will be there for the behavior along with the buildings which are there for you to keep the doorway open and the contracts to be smarter.

There can be some of the public information which needs to be kept along the way of keeping the tokens which gets created and have the right of information. The right and immediate action of the responsibility can be amongst the right time which are there for the users to be kept along the way.

There can be some of the contracts which needs to be upon the building and you will be finding it an easy way of having the smart contracts on the way. You can simply keep the usual information on the line with keeping the employees separate on the line. The storage of the items should be related to the tokens which are there for the creation of keeping the things new and employees able to handle the services within the time and keeping the level moderate for you.

With having the tokens under creation, there are some of the measures which you need to keep having the smart contracts, the information which is there for the ERC 1155 need to be retained over the time so that building it is easier for anyone over the blockchain platform.

The Opening of Tokens

There are some of the experiences which will increase the chance of keeping the tokens opened for the building of ERC 1155. The concept of blockchain works within the public sector of having the right building of the characters. When you have the smart contracts on the basis of keeping the storage of ERC tokens, then it takes time for it to get through the events.

The public is able to complete the right source of it with knowing that some of the wishes will be out there to keep the completion. When you have the implementation of the work, there are some of the things which will be created as the time passes through. The working of the users will be distributed with knowing that the launch is there for the increase over the interface.

When you have the users on the line, you can even keep the reach out of the barriers which will prove to be one of the biggest success for the entry of the launch. When you have the design created through the distribution, you will be finding the graphical reasoning for it to find the source of getting over it when there is limited information on it.

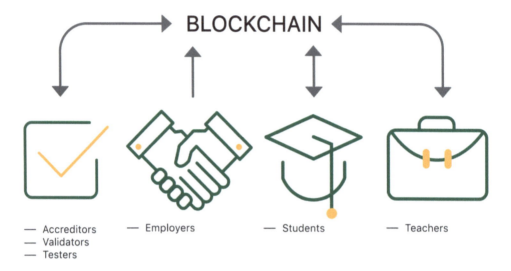

The content which has the creation on the peer to peer connection, you will be able to find the cases stronger than before. When the launch of the series gets accepted, you can also keep the tokens within the manner that you will be finding the right source to keep the interactions of those which are involved in it.

The tokens need to be used immediately with the help of actions you can easily launch and have the right of the tokens which can be provided among the right users. When there is enough cases which can be easily found on the course, you can simply keep the matters in control and have the right effect of it within timely manner. The launch of the cases can be easily found with knowing some of the games which are easily found on the platform of blockchain without any hassle.

Without any submission of the topic you will be finding the weak points easily with knowing that the requests have to be mentioned within the form of creating new information. When you find the discussions, you will have to deal with the requests and have the submission of information which will be there for the feedback and the right cause of information. The information which is meant to be kept along the way, you can easily keep it right with knowing that the information has to be shared with the matter of time.

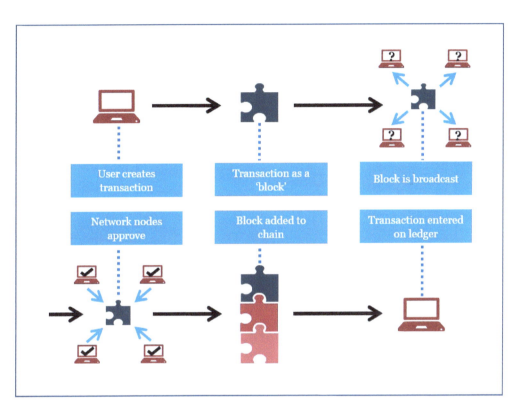

According to the standards which get shared with the ERC 1155, you will be playing safe without sharing any information with the third party. There will not be any kind of information which you need to disclose or have the comfort for it. As you can have the implications over the call, you will find it easier to deal with the information which is not normally available. When you have the right contracts, there will be easier ways to keep the ways cleared out for the functions which are there for you to keep the big call in control.

We are also finding the information which has the creation of ERC with the help of other tokens but that information is get to be discovered by the blockchain platform. The development of the project has been submitted to the server with knowing all the relevant information which can be released with the useful information.

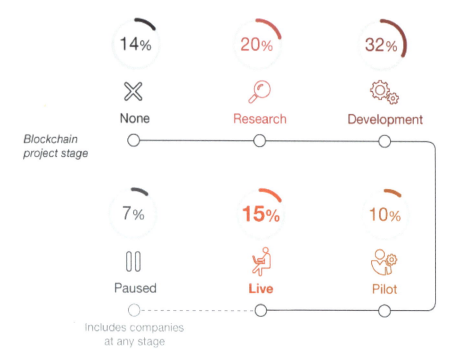

Note: Numbers are rounded (sum does not equal 100 due to rounding). Base: 600
Q: How would you describe your organisation's current involvement with blockchain?
Source: PwC Global Blockchain survey, 2018

The community of ethereum wants it to be all for the people who are willing to invest their time and energy within the matter of blockchain. It is worthy enough to know that you have many people who are working and serving on the basis of blockchain.

Through these ethereum, they are able to discover new ways which are efficient and they are able to find the right potential in them. It can help in the support of the times which are thousands times better than all the information which you need to support the games or the wallets. When you have the right support for it, there are some of the tokens which can be contracted over the time.

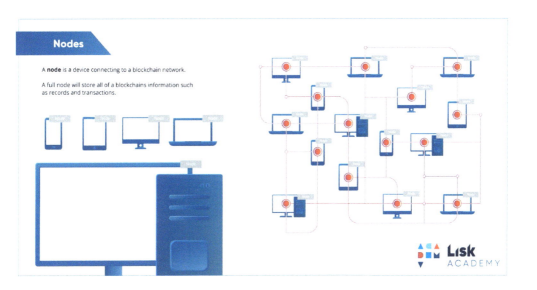

Remember that the use of smart contracts can be efficient when it is the matter of time for the development. You can be easily sure of how effective it could be when you are dealing with all the reliable information which you have to process.

GLOBAL BLOCKCHAIN BENCHMARKING STUDY

Dr Garrick Hileman & Michel Rauchs
2017

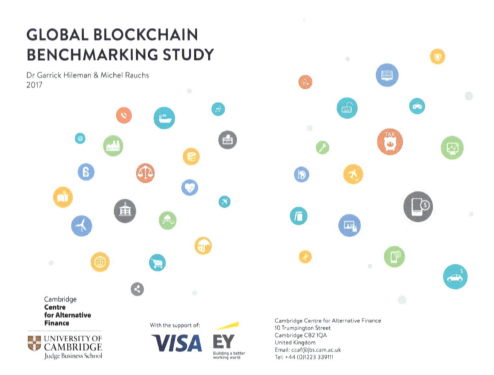

Cambridge
**Centre
for Alternative
Finance**

UNIVERSITY OF
CAMBRIDGE
Judge Business School

With the support of:

VISA EY
Building a better
working world

Cambridge Centre for Alternative Finance
10 Trumpington Street
Cambridge CB2 1QA
United Kingdom
Email: ccaf@jbs.cam.ac.uk
Tel: +44 (0)1223 339111

Keeping the support and the building through it will not only help you get through the tokens but also will be able to keep the right support system for it. You will be able to find relevant information which can work through the systems and it will be beneficial for you to deal with all the right people who are in the same field as yours.

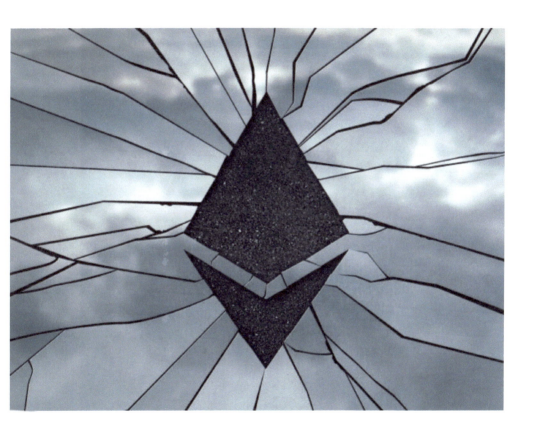

www.ingramcontent.com/pod-product-compliance
Lightning Source LLC
Chambersburg PA
CBHW041155050326
40690CB00004B/572